D1011159

# Disney

# PRINCESS

# TOP 10s

# FROM ARIEL
# TO RAPUNZEL

JENNIFER BOOTHROYD

LERNER PUBLICATIONS ◆ MINNEAPOLIS

Lerner Publications Company
A division of Lerner Publishing Group, Inc.
241 First Avenue North
Minneapolis, MN 55401 USA

For reading levels and more information, look up this title at www.lernerbooks.com.

Main body text set in ITC Avant Garde Gothic 13/14.
Typeface provided by International Typeface Corp.

**Library of Congress Cataloging-in-Publication Data**

Names: Boothroyd, Jennifer, 1972– author.
Title: Disney princess top 10s : from Ariel to Rapunzel / Jennifer Boothroyd.
Description: Minneapolis : Lerner Publications, 2019. | Series: My top 10 Disney | Includes bibliographical references and index.
Identifiers: LCCN 2018010735 (print) | LCCN 2018033874 (ebook) | ISBN 9781541543607 (eb pdf) | ISBN 9781541539075 (lb : alk. paper)
Subjects: LCSH: Walt Disney Productions—Juvenile literature. | Pixar (Firm)—Juvenile literature. | Princesses—Juvenile fiction. | Animated films—Juvenile literature.
Classification: LCC PN1999.W27 (ebook) | LCC PN1999.W27 B66 2019 (print) | DDC 791.43/6528621—dc23

LC record available at https://lccn.loc.gov/2018010735

Manufactured in the United States of America
1-45090-35917-7/16/2018

# TABLE OF CONTENTS

# DISNEY PRINCESS MOVIES ARE THE BEST

**BRAVE HEROINES, EVIL VILLAINS, AND CUTE ANIMAL SIDEKICKS.** What's not to love about a Disney princess movie? If you agree, you've come to the right place. This book lists some of the funniest, scariest, and most amazing moments in our favorite princess movies.

When people are choosing their favorites, they are sharing opinions. And people can have different opinions. So the favorites in this book might not be the same as yours. You might think a different line is funnier or a different scene is scarier. And that's great! You'll have a chance to give your opinions at the end!

**IT'S TIME TO PUT ON YOUR TIARA AND EXPLORE WHAT MAKES THESE PRINCESSES AND THEIR MOVIES FANTASTIC.**

# TOP 10 SCARIEST MOMENTS IN *SNOW WHITE*

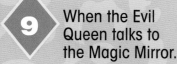

 **10** Entering the Dwarfs' messy cottage.

**ALL THE DUST AND COBWEBS!**

**9** When the Evil Queen talks to the Magic Mirror.

 **8** The Huntsman comes at Snow White with a knife.

 **7** The animals try to save Snow White from the Evil Queen, but she shoos them away.

**6** The Evil Queen tries to stop the Dwarfs with a boulder.

**5** When the Evil Queen dips an apple into the potion, and it looks like a skull.

**CREEPY!**

←

**4** The Evil Queen kicks the skeleton in her dungeon.

**3** When Snow White is lost in the dark forest.

**2** Snow White accepts the poisoned apple.

 **DON'T TAKE A BITE!**

**1**

THE EVIL QUEEN CHANGES INTO THE OLD HAG.

 **OH, THAT CACKLE!**

# TOP 10 MOST CHALLENGING PARTS OF CINDERELLA'S LIFE

**10** Getting only a few minutes of free time.

**9** Walking up all those stairs to her bedroom. **AT LEAST IT'S GOOD EXERCISE.**

**8** Helping her stepsisters get ready for a ball that she's not allowed to attend.

**7** Doing laundry every day.

**6** Protecting her little friends from Lucifer.

## DID YOU KNOW?

Actors were filmed performing many of the scenes in *Cinderella*. Then the animators watched the footage to help them draw the scenes.

 **5** Shoes that fall off too easily.

**SHE LOSES HER SHOE THREE DIFFERENT TIMES!**

 **4** Learning to balance breakfast trays on her head.

**THAT MUST HAVE TAKEN A LOT OF PRACTICE!**

**3** The chiming clock wakes her up from beautiful dreams.

**2** Magic that only lasts until midnight.

**1**

**BEING TREATED LIKE A SERVANT BY HER STEPMOTHER AND STEPSISTERS.**

# TOP 10 REASONS AURORA WOULD BE A FUN FRIEND

**10** It would be awesome to visit her quirky aunts.

**9** The stories about her dreams are so wonderful.

**8** She probably knows where to find the tastiest berries in the forest.

**7** Best karaoke partner ever!

**HER VOICE IS AMAZING.**

**6** She loves going on fun nature walks.

**5** She is kind to everyone.

**4** She has a secret identity.

**KIND OF LIKE A SUPERHERO!**

**3** Her other friends are adorable forest critters.

**2** She loves to dance.

**1**

**SHE HAS A PLAYFUL IMAGINATION.**

11

# THE LITTLE MERMAID'S
## TOP 10 FUNNIEST
## MOMENTS

**10**

Scuttle tries to figure out what is different about Ariel after she's become human.

**SHE'S GOT LEGS, DUDE!**

**9** Chef Louis and Sebastian's chase scene.

**8** Ariel talks to Prince Eric's statue.

**7**

Scuttle tries to hear Prince Eric's heartbeat by listening to his foot.

**6** Prince Eric can barely hold on when Ariel drives the carriage.

**HIS FACE IS PRICELESS!**

**5** Sebastian tries to teach Ariel how to bat her eyelashes and pucker her lips.

**4** Ariel's face when Prince Eric tries to guess her name.

**3** Scuttle tries to sing a romantic song.

**GOOD THING SEBASTIAN TOOK OVER.**

**2** Ariel combs her hair with a fork at the dinner table.

**1** SEBASTIAN AND HIS SEA FRIENDS FINISH THE "UNDER THE SEA" SPECTACULAR ONLY TO FIND THAT ARIEL HAS SWUM AWAY.

# TOP 10 TIMES *BEAUTY AND THE BEAST* TOOK OUR BREATH AWAY

**10** Belle running to the top of the hill and looking out at the incredible view.

**9** The Beast saving Belle from the wolves.

**8** Seeing the library for the first time!

SO MANY BOOKS.

**7**

Belle discovering the magic rose.

SO THAT'S WHY THE WEST WING IS FORBIDDEN.

**6** The Beast deciding to let Gaston go.

 **5** Belle and the Beast dancing in the ballroom.

**4** Belle offering to trade places with her father.

**WOW, SHE'S BRAVE.**

 **3** The Beast becoming human again.

**SEEING EVERYBODY ELSE AS HUMANS IS PRETTY COOL TOO!**

**2** Belle and the Beast seeing each other on the ballroom stairs.

**1**

**THE MOST SPECTACULAR DINNER SHOW EVER!**

# TOP 10 LINES FROM *ALADDIN*

**10**

"Jafar, Jafar, he's our man. If he can't do it, GREAT!" —Genie

**9**

"I must find this one, this diamond in the rough." —Jafar

**8**

"Phenomenal cosmic power . . . itty-bitty living space." —Genie

**7**

"Unhand him, by order of the princess."

**JASMINE BEING A BOSS.**

**6**

"The law is wrong."

**JASMINE BEING UNAFRAID TO SAY WHAT SHE BELIEVES.**

**5** "Do you trust me?"

**HMMM, PRINCE ALI SOUNDS A LOT LIKE ALADDIN.**

**4** "From this day forth, the Princess shall marry whomever she deems worthy."

**SULTAN GIVING JASMINE THE POWER SHE DESERVES.**

**3**

"Ten thousand years will give you such a crick in the neck." —Genie

**2** "Genie, I wish for your freedom."

**ALADDIN IS TRUE TO HIS WORD.**

**1**

**"I AM NOT A PRIZE TO BE WON!" —JASMINE**

# QUIZ BREAK!

How well do you know Disney princesses? Take this quiz and find out!

**1**

### WHICH PRINCESSES HAVE SIBLINGS?

A. Tiana and Merida
B. Ariel and Jasmine
C. Merida and Ariel
D. Cinderella and Tiana

**2**

### WHAT IS THE NAME OF JASMINE'S TIGER?

A. Stripes
B. Abul
C. Rajah
D. Iago

**3**

### WHAT KIND OF PIE IS SNOW WHITE BAKING FOR THE DWARFS WHEN THE OLD HAG APPEARS?

A. gooseberry
B. apple
C. blueberry
D. pumpkin

### WHICH DISNEY PRINCESS IS THE ONLY ONE WHO DOESN'T SING IN HER MOVIE?

**4**

A. Jasmine
B. Mulan
C. Aurora
D. Merida

**5**

**WHO IS THE FIRST ENCHANTED OBJECT TO SPEAK DIRECTLY TO BELLE IN BEAST'S CASTLE?**

A. Chip
B. Cogsworth
C. Lumiere
D. Mrs. Potts

**6**

**WHAT NAME DO THE FAIRIES GIVE TO PRINCESS AURORA WHEN THEY RAISE HER IN THE FOREST?**

A. Mary Blair
B. Briar Leah
C. Briar Rose
D. Mary Costa

**7**

**WHAT DO TIANA AND HER FATHER INVITE THE NEIGHBORHOOD TO TASTE?**

A. gumbo
B. red beans and rice
C. grits
D. corn bread

**8**

**WHAT IS THE NAME OF MULAN'S DOG?**

A. Mushu
B. Little Brother
C. Wanderer
D. Meeko

**9**

**WHAT IS THE NAME OF POCAHONTAS'S BEST FRIEND FROM HER TRIBE?**

A. Kocoum
B. Winona
C. Powhatan
D. Nakoma

**10**

**WHAT WAS THE SOURCE OF RAPUNZEL'S MAGICAL POWER?**

A. an ancient stone
B. a flower
C. an enchanted feather
D. a dragon's claw

# THE TOP 10 THINGS POCAHONTAS MADE US APPRECIATE ABOUT NATURE

**10** Nature isn't just a resource for us to use.

**WE ALSO HAVE A RESPONSIBILITY TO PROTECT IT.**

**9** Trees in the forest can provide shelter and shade.

**8** Nature is a beautiful and colorful place.

**7** The river is perfect for transportation.

**6** Tall trees are great places to check out what's happening.

~ ~ ~ ~ ~
### DID YOU KNOW?
There was a real-life Pocahontas. Her real name was Amonute. Pocahontas was her nickname.

**5** There is always so much more to explore in the wild.

**WHICH RIVER PATH WOULD YOU TAKE?**

**4** Lakes and rivers are great swimming pools!

**3** Animals can be loyal friends!

**2** Going where the wind takes you can lead to amazing places.

**1**

**NATURE HAS A LOT OF ANSWERS IF YOU JUST LISTEN.**

**GRANDMOTHER WILLOW IS SO WISE!**

# MULAN'S TOP 10 "YOU GO, GIRL!" MOMENTS

**10** Mulan keeps training until she can run faster than everyone else can.

**9** She beats Captain Li Shang in their training fight.

**8** When she cuts off her hair with a sword.

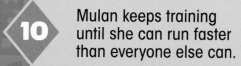

**7** She goes back to warn Shang and the Emperor about the Huns.

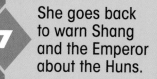

**6** She waits to shoot the canon until just the right moment.

## 5

When she fends off Shan-Yu with only a fan.

**SHE'S GOT SKILLS!**

∧∧∧∧∧

## DID YOU KNOW?

The computer program that artists used to animate large groups of soldiers in *Mulan* is called Attila. It was named after an ancient Hun ruler.

## 4

She decides to protect her father and defend her family's honor.

## 3

She is the first one to figure out how to reach the top of the pole.

**USES HER MIND AND HER MUSCLES!**

└──→>

## 2

The Emperor bows to Mulan (and so does everyone else).

## 1

**SHE SAVES HERSELF AND SHANG FROM FALLING OFF A CLIFF WHILE ON HORSEBACK.**

**CAN'T TOP THAT!**

# TIANA'S TOP 10 ACTS OF PERSISTENCE

**10** She keeps tweaking recipes until they are just perfect.

**9** She works two waitressing jobs to achieve her dream of owning a restaurant.

**8** She encourages Naveen not to give up by teaching him to mince mushrooms.

**SHE KNOWS HE CAN DO THINGS FOR HIMSELF.**

**7** She's not discouraged that the mill is so run down.

**SHE'S GOT VISION! BRINGS IT TO ANOTHER LEVEL.**

## 6

She doesn't fall for Dr. Facillier's offer.

## 5

She learns how to dance.

## 4

She keeps on cooking even when she's a frog.

## 3

She helps Naveen appreciate hard work.

**AND HE TEACHES HER TO ENJOY LIFE.**

## 2

She gets turned into a frog but still works to make her dreams come true!

## 1

SHE LEARNS TO NEVER LOSE SIGHT OF WHAT'S REALLY IMPORTANT.

# RAPUNZEL'S TOP 10 FIRSTS

**10** She saves a life.
**LUCKY FLYNN!**

**9** She makes human friends.

**8** She trains a horse.
**MAXIMUS WOULD DO ANYTHING FOR HER.**

**7** She gets a major haircut.
**AND BECOMES BRUNETTE TOO.**

**6** She swims underwater.
SHE'S A QUICK LEARNER!

**5** She discovers a new way to use a frying pan.

**DID YOU KNOW?**

Rapunzel's chameleon was based on an animator's pet chameleon named Pascal. Chameleons change their coloring to communicate with other animals.

**4** She touches grass.
NOW THAT'S PURE JOY!

**3** She meets her real parents.
SHE'S FOUND PEOPLE THAT TRULY CARE FOR HER.

**2** She stands up to Mother Gothel.

SHE SEES THE LANTERNS UP CLOSE.

# TOP 10 THINGS TO DO WITH MERIDA IN DUNBROCH

**10** Learn some Scottish.
**CRIVENS!**

**9** Listen to King Fergus's stories.

**8** Learn to rock climb.
**MERIDA CAN CLIMB SO HIGH!**

**7** Talk to Queen Elinor about what it was like to be a bear.

**6**

Explore the ancient ruins of Mor'du's lair.

## DID YOU KNOW?

The animators traveled to Scotland to study the country's landscapes and castles. The Standing Stones in *Brave* were inspired by the real-life Calanais Stones on the Isle of Lewis.

**5** Try to keep up with Merida's playful little brothers.

**4** Learn to embroider a tapestry.

**WHAT A BIG PROJECT.**

**3** Ride horses across the open country.

**2** Learn archery.

**MERIDA'S GOT AMAZING SKILLS!**

⟶

**1**

**SLEEP IN A CASTLE.**

# MAKE YOUR OWN
# DISNEY PRINCESS TOP 10!

**PRINCESS LOVERS, THE TIME HAS COME TO CHOOSE YOUR FAVORITES.** Get an adult's help to make a copy of the blank list on the next page. Have a few changes to make to one of these lists? Go ahead! Or even better, create a royal list of your own, such as,

- **TOP 10 REASONS TO TRADE PLACES WITH ARIEL**

Or maybe you can think of the

- **TOP 10 REASONS JASMINE WILL MAKE A GREAT QUEEN**

The sky's the limit!

# MY
## Disney
## PRINCESS
## TOP 10:

10. _____

9. _____

8. _____

7. _____

6. _____

5. _____

4. _____

3. _____

2. _____

1. _____

# TO LEARN MORE

## Books

Hester, Beth Landis, and Catherine Saunders. *Disney Princess Enchanted Character Guide.* New York: DK, 2014.
This guide will help you become an expert on all thing Disney princesses. Discover fantastic facts about the princesses and their friends.

Schuh, Mari. *How to Be a Snow Queen: Leadership with Elsa.* Minneapolis: Lerner Publications, 2019.
Learn what it takes to be a snow queen from your favorite *Frozen* royal, Queen Elsa of Arendelle. Discover how leadership is an important part of her success.

## Websites

Disney LOL: Disney Princess Games
http://lol.disney.com/games/disney-princess-games
Play games with your favorite Disney princesses. Test your puzzle skills or your quick reflexes. Play by yourself, or ask a friend to join.

Disney Princess: Dream Big, Princess
http://princess.disney.com
Explore the worlds of the Disney princesses. Watch videos about how the movies were made. Read their stories. Try a princess-inspired craft or learn to draw one of your favorite princesses.